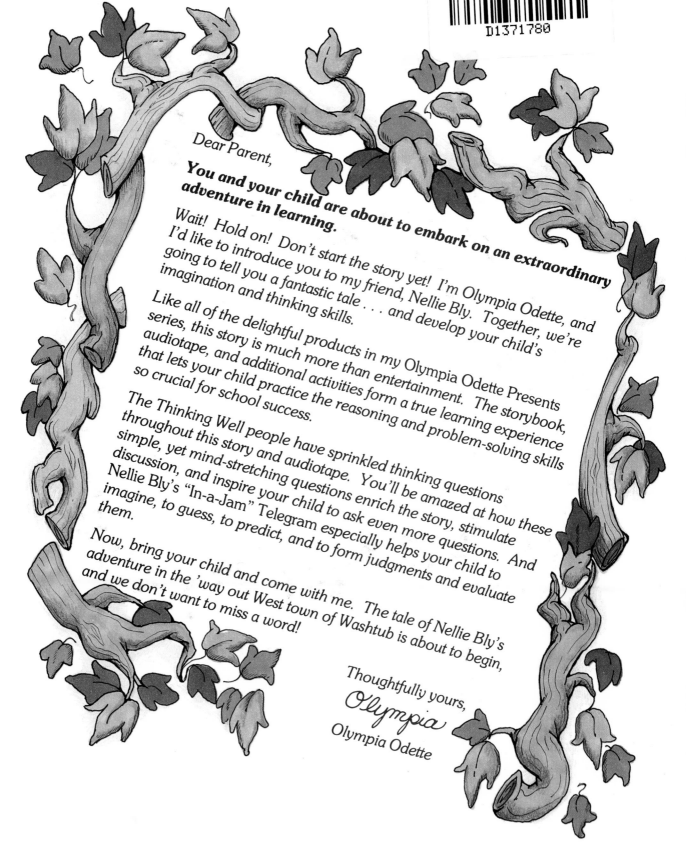

Dear Parent,

You and your child are about to embark on an extraordinary adventure in learning.

Wait! Hold on! Don't start the story yet! I'm Olympia Odette, and I'd like to introduce you to my friend, Nellie Bly. Together, we're going to tell you a fantastic tale . . . and develop your child's imagination and thinking skills.

Like all of the delightful products in my Olympia Odette Presents series, this story is much more than entertainment. The storybook, audiotape, and additional activities form a true learning experience that lets your child practice the reasoning and problem-solving skills so crucial for school success.

The Thinking Well people have sprinkled thinking questions throughout this story and audiotape. You'll be amazed at how these simple, yet mind-stretching questions enrich the story, stimulate discussion, and inspire your child to ask even more questions. And Nellie Bly's "In-a-Jam" Telegram especially helps your child to imagine, to guess, to predict, and to form judgments and evaluate them.

Now, bring your child and come with me. The tale of Nellie Bly's adventure in the 'way out West town of Washtub is about to begin, and we don't want to miss a word!

Thoughtfully yours,

Olympia

Olympia Odette

A division of LinguiSystems, Inc.

Thinking Well
3100 4th Avenue
East Moline, IL 61244

1-800-U-2-THINK

Olympia Odette Presents

Nellie Bly's
"In a Jam" Telegram

Story by Lael Littke
Illustrated by Tom & Carol Newsom

Nellie Bly was the first woman in our country to work as a reporter for a big city newspaper. She was always looking for interesting news to write about. She traveled all over the United States for her stories. One of Nellie's biggest stories took place in the Old West.

What kind of news story would Nellie find in the Old West?

Excuse me! Pardon me, but I want to tell about Nellie Bly and her biggest and best news story. My name is Olympia Odette, and Nellie was a friend of mine. I helped with her newspaper story, and this is the way it happened.

One day I was visiting in a little, Old West town named Washtub. That morning, I noticed the telegraph poles twitching and the telegraph wires whipping around like jump ropes.

I ran as fast as I could to Mr. Pringle's telegraph office. "Mr. Pringle," I puffed, "something mighty strange is going on."

We don't send many messages by telegraph any more. What do we use now when we want to get messages to people fast?

"Goodness sakes! You're right, Olympia. Nellie and I were just puzzling over this telegram."

"Hi, Nellie," I said. "Welcome to Washtub! What's so puzzling about your telegram?"

Mr. Pringle took the telegram from Nellie and gave it to me. I thought it might be full of dictionary-buster words, like the ones Nellie always used. But what it said was, "HEWER EAR SETOH SNEW STEROSI EW NEST OYU OT TEG?"

What do you think happened to the words?

"This doesn't make any sense!" I said. "These jumbled words are as confusing as the twitching telegraph poles! And speaking of confusing, why are **you** here in Washtub, Nellie? I thought you were in New York City writing up stories for that fancy newspaper you work for."

Nellie looked downright worried. "The newspaper sent me here to look for good stories, but I haven't discovered any yet." She stared at the telegram I was holding. "I just received that telegram from my boss, and I can't make any sense of it."

How could Nellie find out what the message says?

Just then the telegraph started chattering like a hundred gazillion woodpeckers on a tin roof. The poles outside started twitching and the wires began wiggling.

Mr. Pringle hurried to write down the new message that was coming in. These words didn't make any sense, either. "All the messages are coming in like that, Olympia," Mr. Pringle said.

I was thinking hard. "Hmmm. I believe the twitching is scrambling up the words, Mr. Pringle." I took another look at Nellie's telegram. "If you untangle all the words, HEWER EAR SETOH SNEW STEROSI EW NEST OYU OT TEG?, it says, 'WHERE ARE THOSE NEWS STORIES WE SENT YOU TO GET?' I think your boss is anxious for you to find something to write about, Nellie."

Why does Nellie's boss want her to send news stories to him?

Nellie took a hankie from her bag and dabbed at her eyes. "What am I going to do, Olympia? Even if there were a gunfight or a train robbery, I couldn't send a telegram to my newspaper—not with words getting all scrambled up like this!"

Mr. Pringle looked like he was about to come down with an idea.

Suddenly he hollered, "Tarnation! There's only one person would pull a stunt like this, and that's Bratley Barfus!"

Bratley Barfus! Of course! Bratley Barfus was an eight-year-old kid like me. He was always inventing goofy things, like the dark bulb. It was like a light bulb, only it made a room dark, even in the middle of the day.

Why hadn't I thought of Bratley?

Is the name Bratley a good name for that boy? Why?

This might be just the story Nellie was looking for. I grabbed her hand and yanked her along after me. We headed for the old schoolhouse Bratley used for his workroom.

When we got there, we found Bratley holding something that looked like an eggbeater. He was turning its handle slowly.

"What do you have there, Bratley?" I asked. He stopped turning the handle of the eggbeater gadget. Just as I suspected, the telegraph poles stopped twitching.

How could Bratley's eggbeater make the telegraph poles twitch?

"Why, it's a telegraph twitcher," Bratley said proudly, holding the gadget up so we could see it. "Why, I was scrambling my eggs one morning when I wondered if I could whip up something that would scramble words. So I made this." He turned the handle on the gadget again, and we watched the telegraph poles start twitching harder than ever.

Nellie looked puzzled. "But why would you want to invent such a thing, Bratley?"

Bratley smiled. "Just for fun, ma'm. I've got all these smarts in my head, and this is the only way I can think of to use them."

Nellie looked around the schoolhouse. She saw fallen-down desks and books covered with cobwebs. "Doesn't your schoolwork keep you busy, Bratley?"

Why do you think Bratley invented the telegraph twitcher?

"Shucks, ma'am," Bratley said, "ain't no schoolteacher wants to come to a dumpy little town like Washtub. We don't have no school. We don't need one, neither."

Nellie gave me a look. "This is a crying shame, Olympia! We must get a schoolteacher for Washtub! Bratley and the other children need to learn things in school to keep their minds growing."

"No such thing," Bratley said. "We young'uns don't want to be cooped up in this here schoolhouse like a flock of chickens, looking at dusty old books."

"But you must have a school and a teacher!" Nellie fished a pencil and notepad from her bag and began to scribble something. "I'll write a story about children being deprived of an education. I'll issue a call for schoolteachers to sacrifice their comfort to bring good school learning to Washtub. I'm going to send my story by telegram to my newspaper in New York City!"

How will a news story help Washtub get a schoolteacher?

Bratley shook his head. "Hmph! I can't make much sense of them fancy words of yours, ma'am, but I do know you ain't sending no telegram." He held up his telegraph twitcher.

But nothing could discourage Nellie. "I **am** going to send a telegram, Bratley! Scramble the words if you like. The people at my newspaper can unscramble them, just like Olympia did!"

Bratley didn't even say anything.   He just turned the handle on that gadget of his so fast it whirred.

The telegraph poles fairly danced, and the telegraph wires snapped around so much, they began to break.   Scrambled words leaked out, piling up in huge heaps wherever the wires were down.

What do you think will happen if all the words leak from the telegraph lines?

Nellie and I watched the stacks of words grow. Every word that had been sent over those telegraph wires was trickling out like water. They were all scrambled up. I saw little words, like ETH, and NAD, and TCA. I saw bigger words, like SHOLOC, and UHOES, and RATIN. I even saw some of those dictionary-busters Nellie used, like PRAGELETH and REFITRON, and when I untangled them, they spelled TELEGRAPH and FRONTIER.

"After all them words leak out," Bratley said, "there won't be none left to write newspaper stories with."

With a cackly laugh he ran outside, turning the handle on his gadget as fast as he could.

"We're going to need a whole school full of teachers," Nellie said. "Some of them can tackle putting something besides mischief into Bratley's head, and some of them can start untangling words."

"But how will we let the teachers know we need them if we can't send telegrams?" I asked.

If they can't send a telegram, how can Nellie and Olympia let teachers know they are needed in Washtub?

"Olympia," Nellie said, "there is more than one way to spread the news. We'll yell a message and ask whoever hears it to yell it on to the next person."

Nellie scribbled out a message on her notepad, and we began yelling it. "EMERGENCY!" we yelled. "NEED SCHOOLTEACHERS IN WASHTUB! ONLY THE BEST! PASS IT ON!"

We yelled it to the north. We yelled it to the south and to the east and to the west. We heard folks yelling it on in every direction.

Nellie sure knew the right words to use. Lots of the schoolteachers thought they were the best, and pretty soon they started coming. Tall, skinny teachers and plump ones came, too. There were good-looking teachers and even some plain ones.

Why do you think so many schoolteachers came to Washtub?

Some of the teachers sat Bratley down and began to teach him math and reading and social science. The tallest teachers reached up and repaired the telegraph wires. The others unscrambled words and took them to the schoolhouse for Bratley to learn to read.

Pretty soon Bratley had so much interesting knowledge in his head that he forgot about things like telegraph twitchers. He began inventing good stuff, like cartoons, and popcorn poppers, and chocolate-covered peanuts!

Nellie wrote up another news story about the twitching telegraph and how good learning came to Washtub. She sent it to her boss in New York City, and he said it was the best story she ever wrote!

I was the one who gave a title to that great story. I called it "If You Can't Send a Telegram, Yell-a-Gram!"

Think 'n' Tell

Would you like to have Bratley Barfus for a friend?   Why or why not?

Bratley Barfus likes to invent things.   Would you like to be an inventor?   What kinds of things would you like to invent?

Have you ever seen telephone lines whip around like jump ropes?   How would you feel if you did?

Nellie Bly was a newspaper reporter. Would you like to be a reporter like Nellie? What exciting events would you like to write about?

Today we send messages by mail or over the telephone.   How would you send a message if the phone lines were down and the post office closed?

Spell a Word

This is a fun game Olympia likes to play whether she's alone or with some friends. You can play it, too!

What you need: pencil   scissors
                     paper   container (with or without a lid)

What to do:

1. Print the alphabet in capital letters on your paper. Space the letters so you can cut between them. Also, be sure to make 3 of each vowel–A, E, I, O, and U.

2. Now cut between the letters so one letter is on each piece of paper.

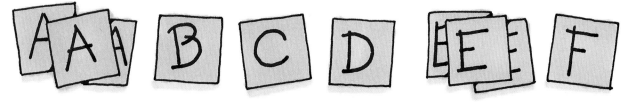

3. Place the letters in the container. Find someone to play "Spell a Word" with you.

4. To play the game, shake the letters in the container to mix them. Then pull out six letters and try to spell a word.   Give yourself a point for each letter you use. Return the letters to the container after each play. The game is over when each player has had 6 turns. The person with the most points wins.

Now you have a game you can take with you when you're on the go. If your container has a lid, you're all set. To make the game even harder, set a time limit for spelling each word. Then shorten the time with each turn. How fast can you spell a word? Can you use all the letters every time? Try to spell different words using the same letters.

How could you use this game to teach people to spell new words? How can you find out if you are spelling your words correctly?

Make a Bookmark

With all the studying Bratley is doing, he needs bookmarks to use at school. You can make bookmarks for all your schoolbooks, too!

What you need: scissors   glue
                               2 colors of construction paper   ric-rac (optional)
                               ruler   pencil

What to do:

1. Cut a piece of construction paper 1½″ x 5″.

2. You can draw your initials in fat letters on this paper or you can cut them out of the second sheet of construction paper.

3. If you have cut out your initials, glue them to the front of the bookmark and let them dry.

4. You can add ric-rac to trim the edges. Just cut pieces of ric-rac to fit the bookmark–1½″ pieces for the top and bottom, 5″ pieces for the sides. Then glue the inside edges of the ric-rac to the back edges of the bookmark.

Now you know how to make bookmarks for a special teacher or for friends. Decorate each one with different objects, such as flowers, animals, rainbows, or clouds. Instead of cutting paper shapes, you can draw them with markers or crayons.

Why do we use bookmarks? What else can you use to mark a page in a book if you don't have a bookmark? What other kinds of bookmarks have you seen?

Jumbled Snack Mix

Olympia needs extra energy for all her adventures. After she helped Nellie Bly solve the jumbled telegram, she created this healthy snack mix to enjoy.

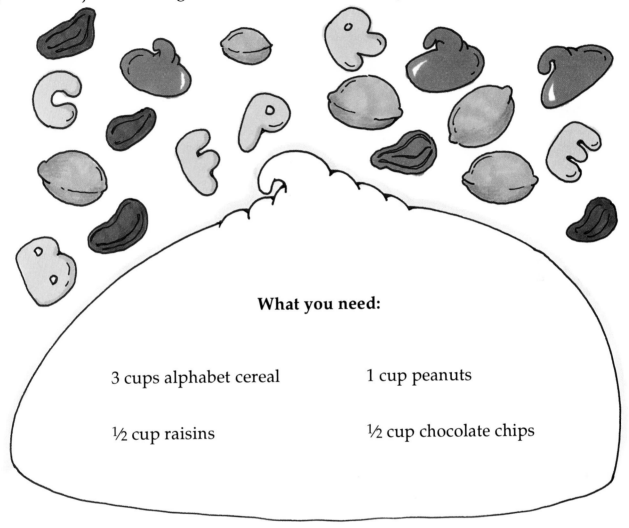

What you need:

3 cups alphabet cereal	1 cup peanuts
½ cup raisins	½ cup chocolate chips

What to do:

1. In a bowl, mix together the alphabet cereal, raisins, peanuts, and chocolate chips.

2. You can add other ingredients that you like. The ingredients in the recipe will give you 5 cups of mix.

Now you are ready to store your mix in a container with a lid, or you can divide it into self-sealing plastic bags. That way you can share your snack with friends or be ready to take some with you on your own adventures.

What would be a good name for this snack mix? Why?
What other quick-energy foods do you like?

The Nellie Bly Rap

Nellie Bly came to town
Lookin' for stories all around.
She tried to send a telegram.
Couldn't get through, "No way, m'am!"

    Click, clack, rattlesnap!
    The words fall off, and they don't come back!
    Clickety, clackety, telegraph twitched,
    Words mixed!   Gotta be fixed!

Bratley Barfus, Twitcher Man,
Mixed up the words and he'll do it again!
Bratley Barfus, put your twitcher away.
Y'oughta be learnin' on a school day!

    Chorus

Olympia told Bratley, "No, no, no!
We've got a message to go, go, go!
Bratley Barfus, you go to school,
Or you'll grow up to be a fool!"

    Chorus

'Scrambled words are hard to read,
Like 'speedle sap' for 'appleseed'.
So Bratley Barfus, hear us shout!
This telegram MUST go out!"

    Click, Clack, rattlesnap!
    The words fell off, but now they're back!
    Clickety, clackety, telegraph twitched,
    Words mixed up.   Now they're fixed!